I WATCH YOU DISAPPEAR
FERANMI ARIYO

This is a work of fiction. All names, characters, places, and incidents are a product of the author's imagination. Any resemblance to real events or persons, living or dead, is entirely coincidental.

Published by Akashic Books
©2024 Feranmi Ariyo
ISBN: 978-1-63614-220-3

All rights reserved
Printed in China
First printing

Akashic Books
Instagram, X, Facebook: AkashicBooks
info@akashicbooks.com
www.akashicbooks.com

African Poetry Book Fund
Prairie Schooner
University of Nebraska
110 Andrews Hall
Lincoln, Nebraska 68588

TABLE OF CONTENTS

Preface by Saddiq Dzukogi 5

My Father Undoes Darkness 9
Cancer Wards 12
Healing 15
He Reads a Cancer Booklet 16
Fission 18
The Last Smoke 20
If One Must Hope 21
My Father Dies 24
... And Goes to Heaven 25
Or Hell? 27
For the People Who Console Us with Psalms and Homilies 28
I Watch You Disappear 30
Half-Life 31
Preface to My Leaving 32

Acknowledgments 34

PREFACE
by Saddiq Dzukogi

In a wistful medley of poems, Nigerian poet and editor Feranmi Ariyo has crafted a profoundly tender chapbook that explores the intricate landscape of illness. *I Watch You Disappear* offers a poignant exploration of emotional turmoil, the fragility of healing, and the undeniable presence of mortality. This collection weaves a lush narrative that captivates with effective metaphors, inviting readers to contemplate the complex interplay between suffering and beauty. It emphasizes that even in the most challenging circumstances, moments of wonder and grace can emerge. Within these moments, there is a recurrent flicker of hope, depicted as a vital lifeline amid the uncertainties of medical challenges.

Ariyo courageously grapples with the inherent difficulty of naming or fully comprehending death, ultimately coming to terms with its elusive nature. The poet acknowledges that attempts to define or grasp the essence of death are often futile, echoing the theme of existential contemplation that runs through the chapbook. With introspective language, he invites us to be immersed in the agonizing landscape of grief. Here, we confront the ineffable nature of death, as the poem(s) grapples with the idea of death as an indefinable concept that cannot be fully understood.

In the poem, "My Father Undoes Darkness," which implies resilience and determination in the face of adversity, Ariyo skillfully employs vivid and evocative imagery to convey emotional depth. Descriptions such as "tumor in his lungs, punctuating the darkness" and "cancer cells look[ing] like contiguous stars" are striking, creating a stark contrast between the beauty of visual metaphors and the harsh reality of disease. The multilayered emotional narrative juggles a sick father's stoicism and a mother's tears of vulnerability, all punctuated by their children's innocent curiosity. The poem captures the raw emotions that arise when facing the possibility of losing a loved one. In "Healing," he writes:

> There is some miracle in gamma light
> that can purify the forms of darkness we nurse beneath our skins.
>
> There are pills to teach the flesh to carry its contents with mercy.
> And there is some therapy in the way a woman palms the temples
> of her son, pleading cancer away with prayers and Psalms.

There is a haunting way in which this poem explores the concept of healing, a healing that relies on prayers and medicine, as well as the collective hands that seek to nudge the body and spirit toward restoration. This show of remarkable depth and introspection captures the essence of human vulnerability and resilience.

The poem begins with a striking image of "amber vials" as a metaphor for the means by which we seek to rid ourselves of the "strange occupations" that afflict our bodies and minds. This emblematic journey continues with the mention of gamma light, symbolizing the miraculous potential of light to purify the darkness that lingers within us. It conveys a peculiar sense of compassion and gentleness in the face of suffering, where a mother's loving touch and prayers attempt to ward off cancer, highlighting the power of human connection in times of distress. A poem of spiritual rites, solace is begotten through faith and traditions, and the words of these rituals infuse the speaker with new life, often just with the simple optimism that tomorrow will be a better day.

This is a poet trained in the composition of rhythm. The repeated phrase, "for thine is Life," reinforces the idea that life is a gift, and healing, in all its forms, is an affirmation of that gift. This repetition, borrowing self-consciously from the archaic idiom of the King James Bible, creates a sense of cadence and ritual, echoing the consideration of faith and healing.

In the heartbreaking poem, "I Watch You Disappear," Ariyo illustrates that when the specter of impending grief casts its shadow, long before the final farewell, one must gather inner fortitude. The poem begins with a striking assertion: "Your dying is a science and I watch it." This opening line sets the stage for a contemplative examination of the physical and emotional aspects of mortality. The speaker observes the inner workings of the body as it revolts against itself, describing the smaller stars of pain and suffering that awaken within the afflicted body. This cosmic metaphor creates a sense of vastness and inevitability, emphasizing the relentless progression of illness:

> I bear witness to your execution, to the carnage
> of smaller stars coming awake in the dark cosmos
> of your body—flaming hotter and hotter until it is almost
> possible to feel each ember, to point to where
> each lump exists in the geodes of your skin.
> ("I Watch You Disappear")

In this heart-wrenching realization, there is an acceptance of the inevitable as "the long obedience of [the speaker's father's] body comes to an end" and the speaker finally declares, "I carry you with me." Ariyo's work is a testament to the power of poetry to explore the depths of human experience. The eloquent language and profound insights in this chapbook offer readers a journey through the complexities of illness, mortality, and the enduring resilience of the human spirit.

MY FATHER UNDOES DARKNESS

I
The first time my father speaks of his cancer
is to my mum, on a Christmas Eve, just days after
he learns of it. Ma sits beside him, swirls the leftover wine.
Malik and I shuttle between peeking between the dusty louvers
and wrestling thin velvet curtains as they flutter like homeless
spirits in incoming harmattan wind.
But he does not tell us that he is sick because we are
still young, or we just would not understand
that he might die, *but not for sure, but likely*. Certainly, not yet.

II
During his annual examination, a doctor films my father's
body for evidence that death exists
there in some form, somewhere, anywhere,
pouring from his veins into the secret places of his body;
the way daylight would poke its soft-tined fingers though stained glass.
The camera finds a tumor in his lungs, punctuating the darkness,
posing like the sun in those 60s Polaroid photographs:
lonely, prodigal, spilling its lights into a dark nimbus of ether.

III
Father says, *chemo . . .* says, *small cell . . . nothing a few doses
of Taxol would not solve*; Mother replies, *You're lucky, you know?
Most people never get to know this early*— just as much
solace as you could glean off a doctor's ceremony of platitudes:
*there is still hope, you just might cut off a few limbs, invent new lungs,
survive the twenty-something side effects of these 3 drugs
[you know your measly, barely above minimum wage, income cannot afford.]
But there is still hope.*

IV
They go quiet for minutes—the kind that often ushers
in a great misfortune. Like in American horror movies.
My mother sobs into her palms, not she like used to
on those nights when he bruised her.

When they come in, they are both silent, their faces etched
with the same expressions of grief, so that it is impossible
to tell which of them is actually sick or suffering.

V
A second scan comes months (probably weeks) later.
This time, professional eyes tell him, *There is nothing conclusive yet.*
At home, my father compares both scans, with the devotion
of meteorologists, climatologists, the ones that keep track of
receding coastlines or forest fires in the Amazon.

And *there is nothing conclusive yet.* No observable change
but the constant weight loss, the air dancer walk he does—his arms
flailing in still air, the emesis, the occasional bleeding,
and fever that make him quit his job.

VI
And finally, my father undoes darkness. This night he raises the
PET scan higher than he has ever before. It is the way a priest
would lift a goblet of hard bread or the red wine of sacrament
before communion.

Cancer cells look like contiguous stars, to me. Malik yells, *stars*;
my mother chuckles at this, then segues back into crying.

There are so many names for dying, not one way to define
what is truly alive.

I try to make a shape of these prodigal lights, but nothing forms.
Nothing ever does.

I had never imagined death, never imagined it would be
an elegant display of crafts of fire—galactic sparks no skies
would dare to keep. A portrait of their rapture. Each body of light
meaning just a little more than wild flares let loose to disrupt
the darkness my father gathers in his body.

CANCER WARDS

... a rotating cast of characters in various states of tumor-driven unwellness. Why did the cast rotate? A side effect of dying.
—John Green, The Fault in Our Stars

I
The old woman on the other side of the narrow corridor
asks why you are here. *Which are you*, she asks, *sick person or loved one?*
When she speaks with slurs, it reminds you of Aunt Mathilda.
And you say something to her, about tumors spinning
in your father's lungs.
Their Manifest Destiny—a holy war of spreading a gospel
of lethal light across the muck of his flesh.

She tells you about therapy—a weekly fellowship
of suffering for women with bodies on fire.
What is therapy anyway? Something like this?
The way we find pleasure in communion
with another body that equally understands pain?

She speaks of the *reckless constellations* that burn her breast.
She takes out an ultrasound from her purse, creates meaning
off the monochrome scrawls.
Years of reviewing scans have made her a scholar
(You are just in your first few weeks, still learning the
silent cartography of death.)
She says it is her grandson in a womb. *That is his leg and that is his head*
—the ethereal blackness where his eyes and nostrils
would come to occupy, but you don't see anything.

With her, you learn that everything means something.
The dark corners, the gray scrawls mean something,
mean the child's cells, too, are spreading, but in a good way,
in a different way from which her cancer tumbles
a few feet down, spreads, scalds more parts of her body.

When she cups her hands around still air, cradles it
like a metaphor, says she might never get to cradle
her grandson in this way, all you do is apologize.

II
She comes, she goes.
She comes, and goes.

But weeks earlier than prophesied, when she disappears,
all the nurses deny her whereabouts;
your father opines that she has moved away to some
faraway clinic because denial is the only
way he knows can soften
the idea that she no longer exists.

III
When your father gets worse, at first, it's scans, cotton swabs, brown
antiseptics, preternaturally long needles that pierce his spine. And then,
it's waiting for some other person to die or leave somehow because there
are no empty beds.

It's stethoscopes, blue bedspreads, an awful number of colored pills.
Poorly spiced hospital food. It's waiting in the lobby, the panic attacks
every time the doctors step out, the way your eyes follow them as if trailing a plane crashing a few miles ahead. It's scrubs and purple gloves. The

same questions a hundred fucking times. The occasional new discovery
by another attending, the half comforts of survival reduced to percentage.

A 3 a.m. cry. A man unconscious, intubated, who never wakes up all
the while your father is sick; his wife who comes to cry or to speak of
pictures of their daughter in college.

Your crying aunts that make your father cry with a tube in his mouth. A
family to which visiting hours do not apply. Blood pressure charts. The
constant blip of vitals. The pneumonia you never paid for but got anyway. The two doctors conspiring behind the curtain to tell your mother
something perturbing enough to make her drive off to a nearby bar. The
night when you saw her crying in chapel even though she said she was
just going to pee.

IV
Once, when the older nurse asks you to wait in the lobby,
you meet a mother and her daughter who is too young
to be dying but is. You want to speak with her, but the
only way you know to start these conversations is to ask,
Which are you, sick person or loved one? But the answer is right
there; the answer is her head sheared to the scalp.
You know there are fires somewhere in her body, and
all you want to do is hug them to sleep.

Today you learn a lesson or two on simultaneity.
How to inhabit multiple spaces at once—your *cancertastic* present
and alternate futures where she survives, where your father
survives; where she moves to become a doctor or to teach first grade
mathematics in some remote space of Ishinomaki or
Willunga or Malindi or Venice.

HEALING
After Kechi Nomu

Sometimes, amber vials are the only way to rid the body of its
strange occupations. There is some miracle in gamma light
that can purify the forms of darkness we nurse beneath our skins.

There are pills to teach the flesh to carry its contents with mercy.
And there is some therapy in the way a woman palms the temples
of her son, pleading cancer away with prayers and Psalms.
*Don't we sometimes touch each other to free the other from things
that should not be here?*

And then, kneeling on the stairway to an altar is another way to
pacify the carnage of death. There is a ritual with oils pressed out of
the olives of Gaza, waters hallowed by French ornaments, lights
stained by church glass.

There is the baptism of words, when scriptures creep
into our skins as if we are empty pages. And there is a balm in
Gilead, a way to return the body in installments—body parts
subtracted, served up as living sacrifice to pacify the Lord's loneliness.

For thine is the kingdom.
For thine is the body.
For thine is Life
For thine is Life
For thine is Life

HE READS A CANCER BOOKLET
After Carrie Shipers, "He Watches the Weather Channel"

There is nothing more important
than to know which brand of death is killing him.
He needs something to translate the gibberish
of scientists into gibberish that he can understand.

It is also important to know the inner mechanics
of things, like the body, his body—how
at some point, it grew tired of putting all the lights out.

It is hard to say why only he, of all the smokers behind
the bombed mosque, was given the plague of decaying lungs,
and why no one has told him why the drugs aren't working.

He learned that cancer is not some stranger,
but a carnage of his own invention, his burnt cells now
comminatory, now so passionately devoted to tearing him apart.
He wonders if they still have any pity in doing their jobs.

There is still no cure for a metastasized cancer,
but my mother constantly natters about dead prophesies
of black seed, about some guy who met some other guy
who was saved from a stage 4 by a self-invented therapy
of hot lemonade, unripe pineapples, mashed cloves, and vitamins.

Every drug trial that fails or is inconclusive is
one that would not save him.

He just wants to be alive, but there is nothing
left to do; and there is nothing he can change.
Uncertainty aches worse than the cancer,
worse than all the chemo, worse than dying.

FISSION

Death is not a design, not an idea. Death is the body, I know this now, it's your arms . . . It is the whole of us, only we walk around enough to think it isn't.
—Matthew Dickman

I
When my aunt falls sick, her prodigal arms sketch strange sermons
in the air; her *frictioning* joints lisp broken psalms into
our ears, into this poem. And everything about Huntington's says something,
says the body is threatened by chaos, errant pathways of neurons
firing repeatedly, her fingertips play pizzicati on invisible stings.

II
And one night, after the rain, my father bends at the door for minutes
with drenched clothes fastened to his flesh.
He pants out the words: *I'm sorry, despite all the medicine, they spread.*
He holds up a scan and it becomes a photograph of dark clouds.
You could almost hear the scrabbling of exile and of small stars in his body—
which are actually tumors burning, getting comfortable with being lost
as if banishment were immutable to their existence.

III
Here's the thing: fission does not begin when a father holds a scan
speckled with the gleam of small explosions. It's a delicate process—
the body expiring, the intricate design of it: cells chugging on their suicide vesicles
without argument, blood vessels giving up their elasticities,
or telomeres untwining in perfect obedience to the secret Latin of rot.
Entropy is simple and complex, just as jagged street rocks. We are ductile
things chiselled by the same wild winds that drive the vanes of clocks.
Fission does not end when a son hides the ashes of his father
in churning water or gives his body whole to worms.

Death is not an emergency but the body limping against its own walls as it realizes freedom.

THE LAST SMOKE

And once, after we learn that he is never going to recover,
my soon-to-be-dead father asks for a cigarette. Like
kids wailing for candy in places where they do not exist—
the body's thirst for things it knows cannot be.
This is in the car at night. We're past the old overpass,
past the old factory where he once miraculously turned hot metal
into steel bars, blocks, rods . . . every day.
We are past all the liquor stores, into the congregation of soft wood—
often noisy at this time of the day,
the nigh infinite darkness that pulls us closer to the promise of home.
This is after some sixty weeks of ending his dependency,
and now we know for certain that he is going to die.
I can tell that mother is angry but mostly surprised.
"There are no stores around," she says, and he says, "I know."
But we drive back to get it for him anyway.
The worst days are already here.
He doesn't even smoke much.
He throws the cigarette out the window not even minutes
after he lights it.
It must be the false utopia of our minor victories. Like a life jacket
given to a drowning man at the heart of a sea or
the proverbial rich man getting a drop of water in hell.
There was no more risk anyways. To smoke on bad lungs
is to throw a tinderbox into bush fires. *It's a metaphor,*
I guess!
You put the killing thing right between your teeth,
now that it can no longer kill you,
not any faster, not any worse, not any more.

IF ONE MUST HOPE

Enough with the foolishness of hope... If one must pray, I imagine it is most worthwhile to pray towards endings.
—Hanif Abdurraqib

I
Through the transparent walls
of hospital rooms, it is easy to discern
which incarnation of death waits eagerly,
like it, too, is family.

Through them, it is easy to witness the fold of men bound
around the refectory table of a rented bed, dining on an unholy
communion of suffering.

And it is also easy to get electrified by the way florescent lights
flood the scene of yet another mother who can no longer bleed
as she numbers the beads that suspend the Cross on her Rosary.
How she strokes the thinning hair of her only child
as his life grows more monstrous with time.

Her mind is so used to joy so that when it is lost,
she is willing to be brutalized by the hope of its return.

For this same reason, despite being sure that Pa would die,
my mother still kisses soft prayers into Saint Peter's toes,
a petition for reprieve, begging for grand exceptions
to be granted.

But hope is a plot device
for the story ahead of us,
which we can hardly touch

but try to anyway.

Death ignores our bribes of
tubers of yam and prayers mailed to God,
repeating things that He has always known.

II
One night, in the ward, I cling to my father's
whittled arms while I sit beside him, listening to a refrain
of sounds pour like silent prayers from his lungs.
At this point, his chest becomes
too reluctant to fold any more air—a side effect of the cancer,
of bearing a set of genomes carefully decapitated by burning tobacco.

And Ma sits beside me all night, intoning
Psalms, litanies about jars of ink, miles of pages
invested in God's inventory of hairs—
when my father has no hair,
which is a side effect of all the chemo—
trading body parts for a few more days
to refuse God's custody.

III
On the next morning, after spasming, my father would
not wake, my mother wails so loud, loud enough to
be mistaken for madness,
then she speaks nothing for days.

The loss of words,
the loss of silence;

side effects of hope—
how, when it's gone, it bruises;

how grief becomes, like faith, the substance
of things longed for but not seen.

But hope is necessary, I've decided,
in the way that for awhile
it keeps the rest of the world sane.

MY FATHER DIES

My mother says no one can fight it —the body returning to God
—Warsan Shire

My father dies on a hospital bed at the end of several
rituals to capture his memories within the soft murals
of his body. It is impossible to tell if he is just spasming
or leaping in excitement (possibly terror) at the sound of a procession
of angels blowing their hallowed horns for the ten-thousandth
time this day—in pitches only the dying would hear.
I don't know how else to say this: there seems to be nothing new
or extravagant about dying, at least to angels, just the sum
of the body's small tragedies, a measure of how much of these
the body would outlast.
While my father dies, my mother strides in with a box of matzos
and freshly baked, sugar-dusted, jam-stuffed doughnuts. The nurses are too
busy wrestling death in an absurd tug-of-war in which my father is just
one rope, the other being the tendrils of a defibrillator stretched out
to spasm him even more, to keep him alive. But nothing seems
to be sufficient to do this:
not the 200 volts jolts wading fervently to save his heart or the 2 mLs
of epinephrine stabbed into his varicose veins; not my mother wailing
in falsetto, *let me see . . . let me see him,*
as she gets hauled away by frustrated ward maids;
not the collage of mashed donuts—their gooey strawberry jam now
patching the clinic floor like a *red vine of blood.*
And death, *the grim reaper herself,* the always so immediate becomes even more
immediate. Dressed in black, steel chains swaying around her neck, she cranes
over his bed as if caring but holds the bloodied sickle in her hands
with which she pulls him, pulls us. But we do not follow.

. . . AND GOES TO HEAVEN
Our Father, who art in heaven, hallowed be thy name.

My father boats over milk and honey, over the slow waters
of Hiddekel for what might be forty minutes or forty days,
and no one can tell because time remains un-demarcated.
He remains fifty-whatever forever,
the strings of thin grey hair are now as immortal as he is.
His gut is always slightly hollowed from the violent emesis.

He and I must now exist in separate places.
Day is still for him, illumined by the Son's holy light
and all the lights my father takes from us, while I remain brutalized
by false midnights on a sheet and wild stars sprinkled over PET scans.
It is in loss that we learn the fluctuant mechanics of time, how
it could bend to will—so that every night could be the night just before
my father dies—if I want it to.
And morning would meet him dead again.

I think of the burst of incandescence in his body and its fidelity
to the lethal gesture of motion—as if aching for something beyond.
I suppose it is possible to think of this as proof of an afterlife.

I think of the tender pull of age, not as slow as I want it to—bringing
us all to the promise of extinction.

I think of heaven as a place filled with people condemned to be happy.
Like an eternal last night of summer camp —people chanting,
hovering around fires without tiring, or a pub
with all the free booze one could ask for.

My father's lips are silent. They can never cry out.
It is I who must grieve his death in his stead because no one
can weep in heaven.
It might take sixty days or sixty Earth-years, but I believe
my father would get tired of the utter tedium of constancy.
He would notice that even opalescent gold and polished
stones lose their willingness to dazzle after long.

He would learn why saints and angels, alike,
herald the arrival of the dead [something new at the least],
singing Glory.

*Glory of light. Glory of fires, Glory of the things
they leave behind. Glory of brevity, of all things that pass away.
Glory of the forgiveness that death procures. Glory of our fathers,
now in heaven, their sins forgotten, their wills still done on earth,
their names hallowed by death.*

OR HELL?
After Megan Fernandes

We drink freshly made lemonades and you say something about
the Tuskegee Experiments, the dismal science of the castrati,
or how women were once set aflame for refusing to drown,
and that this world could be punishment enough if one is born
in the wrong cities, the wrong bodies, or wrong centuries.
Your eyes are tired from watching all of god's shortcomings.
So, we mostly speak of perfect things that we cannot really have.
I tell you that for once, I agree with the Witnesses, that Hell could be
a metaphor [for here], for everything outside of god
[and god, according to some, is an old white man],
for that kind of pain which no one could see you wrestle
a force not quite knowable or nameable.
And that we invent heaven as reward for the unhappy business of living.
But you believe in an afterlife.
You say what's the point of our existence, of thousands of
years of creation, of giving decades of our lives to this world
of angry men if we could so easily be eliminated.
But I know that you only believe because you are tired, sad that this
could be all to our presence, that the woes are multiplying
faster than the words to describe them. So you are willing to be
fiddled by a promise of something more, something better, or perfect.
I tell you that this is all the hell there needs to be;
that our fathers were burning long before they ever lit cigarettes;
that we, too, are burning men;
that death is where their suffering ends and ours begin.
For there is no work, nor knowledge, nor wisdom, in the grave.

FOR THE PEOPLE WHO CONSOLE US WITH PSALMS AND HOMILIES
After Danusha Lameris, "The God of Numbers"; after Darren Morris

How hard we try to break the world down, make sense of it. How steadily it resists.
—Danusha Lameris

I
Before the flood, there were lots in the uttermost part of the earth
who would not believe—not God—but some village
recluse who claimed he could now hear Him.
And that it was by God's Divine Will that the world would be purged in a
baptism of rivulets.
And there were women who were not willing to be banished—away from families,
from decade long careers into some untested utopia, which was actually
a wooden arc that Noah had spent a reasonable twelve decades
shoving all kinds of beasts into.
And there were children dancing arounds mats in a park who could barely
hear or recognize that the rain could be God's wrath collapsed
into something tangible, or that the rainbows that came after
would be an extravagant display of a war crime.
But then, *a rose survives the flood and suddenly,*
God is innocent again.

II
You claim there is God in the small things, say he is—for some
reason—romantically invested in the minutiae of things: the number
of our hairs, the tributaries of axons sprouting out the trees of our nerves.
That He keeps some kind of record of them. And when you tell me,
everything happens for a reason, I know that cancer, sometimes, is the wages
of our transgressions, the body's iniquities given life—*Mene, mene, tekel*...

I have seen my father sit on the other end of cigarette fires, burning
wounds, sealing the grief that seeped out of his flesh until his body
began to blossom with flowers of light.

III
Everyone wants speak about god. And I, too, like to imagine that god
who keeps an inventory of hair loss on stone tablets,
keeps a record of the feathers of doves, the migration routes
of greater flamingos or how they feed. But no one wants
to acknowledge their god as the strange artist that sparks little incendiaries
in the dark ether of their mother's body—who has never
smoked a day. His other acts of creation. The things that happen
on the days after He rested: plagues, fires, and then floods.
But one in ten people survive pancreatic
cancer and suddenly, *God is love* again.

IV
We think of everything as a sign, declare the configuration of luminaries
to mean something exotic about our lives. Say Sagittarius, Taurus, and then
say Cancer. A cancer took my father from us [to heaven].
Men will search for meaning in empty alleys as if one listens hard enough,
the rhythms of distant speech, so much clatter at a distance could not make
a sound close enough to whatever seeks to be heard.
We leverage on the uncertainty of things and call it hope
because it is the only promise that is left.

And even if all of the Precambrian and Phanerozoic could fit into six days,
even if my father was actually sculpted from dust and holy breath,
even if everything happens for a reason—all of that knowledge
would not deny us our suffering.

I WATCH YOU DISAPPEAR

Your dying is a science and I watch it—
the inner workings of a body in its purest revolt.

I bear witness to your execution, to the carnage
of smaller stars coming awake in the dark cosmos
of your body—flaming hotter and hotter until it is almost
possible to feel each ember, to point to where
each lump exists in the geodes of your skin.

On the silent days between each scan, we are transfixed
by a forecast of burning cities in your body.
I watch you disappear, from bleachers into the wards.
I watch you transfigure as the tumors gnaw you away
and the long obedience of your body comes to an end.

I see it cram all the motion of a lifetime into just a few minutes
as if a huge debt of motion had to be paid in such little time.

At your funeral, your body is immobile, wan as the skins
of painted actors playing ghosts in low-budget horror movies.
No polished mahogany lined with soft white, just the fires
of an incinerator wiping you away, burning the cerements,
replacing your skin till you are little enough to hold in an urn.

I carry you with me. Our aunts gather your clothes,
the left-over cereal boxes—what is left of you.
We inherit these and the darkness the fires would not burn,
we inherit the silence of a body no longer occupied
by what we loved.

HALF-LIFE

My mother, at forty-five, sits in the
doctor's office,
inventing evidence to prove pieces of her are getting
hauled away by vandals.
She holds her disfigured skin as she invents new names
to heighten the sting of every symptom of her erasure:
"Back pains"
"Spaghetti veins"
"Callused skin"

I imagine the tired doctor reducing her symptoms,
time after time, to *you're just old* or any other elegant
interpretation of how she atrophies.
And my mother now comes home with
new prescription pills even though now she knows
that there are no more exotic pills to save us,
to delay the epiphany that old things will pass away—
that we are old things.

PREFACE TO MY LEAVING
For Gbenga Adeoba

Strange, the things we find between words, the intimate
spaces where we also hide our fears of inadequacy.

I, too, have learned the alphabets of silence, rented metaphors
to paint portraits of things outside the economy of light.
Things that may never again be seen.

* * *

Tell me, who sits in front of your blank boards?
What things do you paint?

Who is like God? Who says unto himself, *let us make words
in our own image? And poetry after the kinds
of silence we bring to these pages?*

* * *

I give you my voice—the dark vowels,
psalms that cannot be made into songs, strange songs
that are sent to the altar of an imported god.

I bring you to the theater of my existence.
Lately, I have been teaching myself to raise dead people,
to put them on the stages of the rooms I have never left.
I make you sit in the same sofa where I once sat to watch my aunt
dance fervently to the orchestra of nothing.

I unveil my father, the mole on his chin, the bruises on his
wrists from all the phlebotomies and infusions.

I tear his flesh in communion so that you, too, may feast on
the unnameable taste of burning.

I show you my mother—whom I color with gray and all
the other colors of leaving—as a map from which its little
continents of laughter have fallen.

I retell a story with broken lines that may never be stitched
into coherence, a measure of my suffering weighed solely
in metaphors. I make you learn this suffering in the
same dialect in which I learnt it.

And I give you my exile, from which there is no returning,
my rupture and the preface to my leaving.

ACKNOWLEDGMENTS

The closing lines of the poem "Healing" paraphrase the closing lines of "The Hollow Men" by T.S. Elliot.

The closing lines of the poem ". . . And Goes to Heaven" adapt lines of "Glory" by Gbenga Adesina.

The poem "Preface to My Leaving" paraphrases the line "I give you my rain' . . . from which there is no returning" from "Vanishing" by Gbenga Adesina.

The words "It's a metaphor, I guess! You put the killing thing right between your teeth,
now that it can no longer kill you . . ." are adapted from *The Fault in Our Stars* by John Green.

The line ". . . a rose survives the flood and suddenly, God is innocent again" is from "Thorax" by Logan February.

The line "Death is not an emergency" is from "Death Is Not an Emergency" by Carrie Shiper.